celebrate God's mighty deeds

Let us praise and thank the Lord for his love and his mighty deeds. Let us celebrate his mighty deeds in the assembly.

(adapted from Psalm 106 [107]: 31-32)

celebrate God's mighty deeds

Pupil's Text *(revised 1972)*
The Canadian Catechism

PAULIST PRESS

NEW YORK, N.Y.   PARAMUS, N.J.

Griffin house

TORONTO   MONTREAL

Cat. No. 2-100

Celebrate God's Mighty Deeds is the English edition of The Canadian Catechism for 7-8 year olds, written in collaboration with the Office de Catéchèse du Québec, Montreal, the National Office of Religious Education, Ottawa, and the Office National de l'Éducation Chrétienne, Ottawa, Canada.

Approved by the Canadian Bishops
Wilfred E. Doyle, J.C.D., D.D., President,
Office of Religious Education, English Sector,
Canadian Catholic Conference, February 9, 1972
and
Gérard-Marie Coderre, D.D., President,
Office National de l'Éducation Chrétienne, French Sector,
Canadian Catholic Conference, March 6, 1972.

Editorial Team:
French Edition:
Jean-Paul Bérubé (team leader), Marcel Caron, Françoise D'Arcy, Martin Jeffery, Alberte Julien, Renée Dubeau-Legentil, Suzanne Lévesque, Réginald Marsolais, Margaret Ordway, André Turmel, Bruno Vezeau.

English Version:
May O'Hanlon (team leader), Lawrence DeMong, Martin Jeffery.

With the co-operation of the Institut de Catéchèse du Québec, the team working on the primary level of pastoral services for the Catholic Schools of Montreal, and the diocesan offices of religious education of French and English Canada.

Design:
The Studio, 868 Merivale Road, Ottawa.

Illustrations:
Jeanne Courtemanche-Auclair

Printed and bound:
In the United States of America

Photo credits:
Rapho Guillumette Pictures:
  Bob Smith: pp. 8, 33, 50
  Hella Hammid: p. 29
  Bullaty Lomeo: pp. 39, 70
  Susan Johns: p. 53
  Bruce Roberts: pp. 76
  Fred Lyons: p. 74
Antoine Désilets: p. 15
John de Visser: pp. 18, 21, 62
Odon Kovats: pp. 20, 43, 58, 73
Photo-Pic: pp. 22, 23
Paulist Press: pp. 25, 31
Agence Bulloz: p. 36
Keystone Agency: pp. 40
Edmonton Separate School Board: pp. 51, 59
Cefag: p. 67
Neil Holman: p. 64

Published by:
Paulist Press
455 King Street West, Toronto 135, Ontario
and
P.O. Box 153, Station R,
Montreal 326, P.Q.

Copyright:
© 1972 by Office de Catéchèse du Québec, Montreal, Canada. All rights reserved. No part of this book may be reproduced in any form without permission in writing from the publishers.

Acknowledgment:
Excerpts from the Jerusalem Bible Copyright © 1966 by Darton, Longman and Todd, Ltd., and Doubleday & Company Inc., reprinted by permission of the publisher.

ISBN 0 88760 029 8

to parents

This book is a continuation of the catechism *Come to the Father.* Its purpose is to further develop the child's Christian formation by helping him to discover the wonderful things the Lord does for us in the sacraments.

As you leaf through this book, you will notice that its contents are focused on the Eucharist, and that the principal aspects of this mystery are presented in close relationship to the experiences of the child's life.

You may be surprised by one thing: the absence of an explicit catechesis on the sacrament of penance. The presentation of this sacrament has been postponed until a later time for reasons that will be explained to you in the brochure addressed to parents.

However, special care has been taken to deepen the child's moral formation, in order to help him gradually to discover the Christian meaning of penance.

Participation in your parish and regular reading of the brochure prepared for your use will aid you in your efforts to provide for your child the loving and effective presence he has a right to expect of you during this year.

contents

1.

we get acquainted

It is fun to
get to know others.
We learn each other's names
and where we live.
We talk about
what we like to do.
When we work and
play together,
we get to know each other
very quickly.

2.

what joy to have friends

We are happy to play together as friends.
With friends we can share together.
We can do many things together.
We can have so much fun.

3.

Jesus had friends

One day Philip and Andrew
came to Jesus.
He was happy to see them.

Later, Jesus met Matthew and
said to him:
''Come, follow me.''

Lord Jesus,
I would like to be your friend too.

4.

we like to celebrate with our friends

On special days,
like a birthday,
we celebrate with our friends.
At a celebration,
what really matters is
that we are together.
We enjoy one another and we
get to know one another better.

5.

Jesus celebrated with his friends

Do you remember
the wedding at Cana?

Jesus visiting
Bethany?

His Last Supper
with his friends?

We sing:
My soul is longing for your peace,
near to you, my God. (Song 20)

6.

Jesus does wonderful things for me

Water is cool.
Water is good.
Water makes things live.

Jesus wanted me to be baptized with water.
By this sign he tells me:

"I want you to live with a new life,
the eternal life
of the children of God."

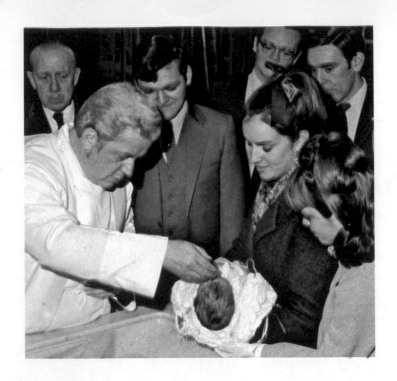

7. Jesus invites me to be his friend

When I was a baby, my parents took me
to church to have me baptized.
They promised to help me know Jesus,
and be his friend.

Now I have grown older
and Jesus asks me:
  "Do you want to be my friend?"

Jesus invites us to the

feast of eternal life

Jesus says to us:
"You are my friends — forever."

(adapted from John 15:14)

Glory to God, Glory.
O praise him, Alleluia.

(Song 21)

at the Eucharist, we celebrate our friendship with Jesus

The children you see
are friends of the Lord Jesus.
They have come to celebrate
the new life, the eternal life
that God gives them.

Christians try to find ways
of always making the Eucharist
a more beautiful celebration.

10.

Jesus is our light

Jesus tells us:
"I am the light of the world;
anyone who follows me
will not be walking in the dark;
he will have the light of life."

(John 8:12)

We sing:
"By his word God enlightens
our hearts, Alleluia!"

(Song 24)

we

28

11.

listen to God's Word

The Lord Jesus says to us:
"You are my friends.
   All that I have heard from my Father
   I have made known to you."
(adapted from John 15:14-15)

Glory be to you, O Lord!
(Song 26)

the Holy Spirit unites us to the Father and to Jesus

The Holy Spirit helps us
to discover the
love of God our Father
everywhere —

> a beautiful landscape,
> a happy family.

Do I ever think about that?

13.

the Holy Spirit teaches us to pray

There are many ways
of praying to God our Father.
We can talk to him in our hearts.

''When we do not know how to pray,
the Spirit himself comes
to help us pray to the Father.''
(adapted from Romans 8:26)

Honor and praise be to the Father,
the Son and the Spirit
world without end.

(Song 6)

15.

we celebrate
the coming of Jesus

Because Jesus has come into the world,
a great light shines in our hearts;
we know that the Father loves us.
Yes, Jesus is really the light of the world.

Glory to God in the highest,
and peace to his people on earth.

16.

we discover the joy of sharing

Getting together is lots of fun!

When we share,
  we are happy.
We make others happy too.

We can share our joy.
We can share our love.

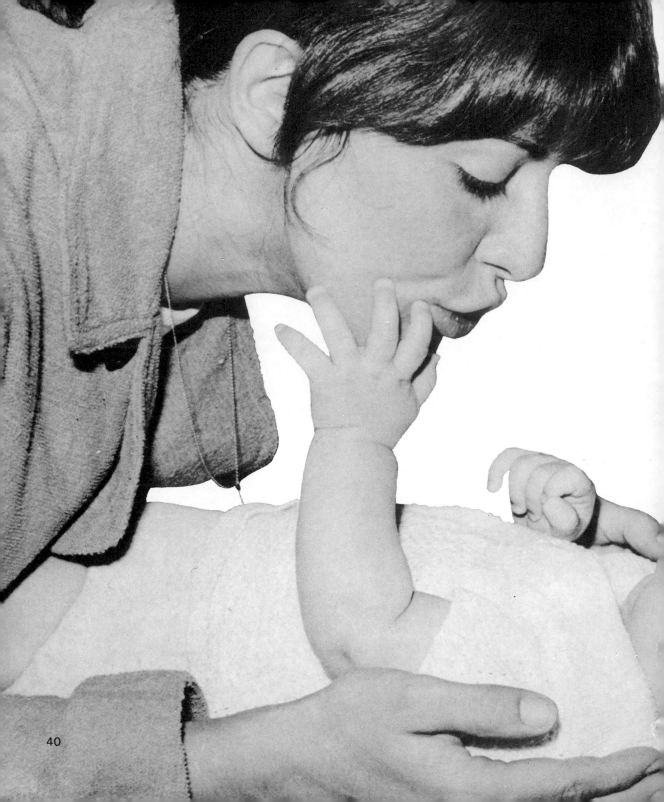

God our Father shares everything with us

''God created all men, he is the one who made them.
He gave them everything that is on the earth.
God wanted men to be like him.
He gave them a little of his power.
He gave them a heart to think with.
He put his own light in their hearts.
And men will tell the mighty deeds of the Lord.''

(adapted from Sirach 17:1-10)

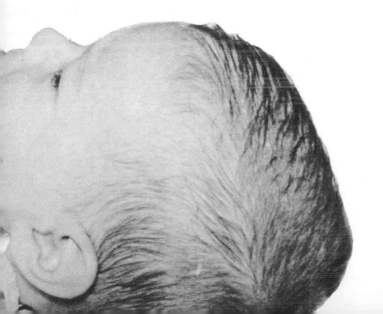

O God our Father,
to share your joy with us
you give us our beautiful world;
you make us able to love and to work;
you give us your Son Jesus
and your Spirit.
We give you thanks
with joyful hearts.

18.

like God his Father, Jesus wants to share his joy with us

Jesus used to meet many people
on the roads of his country.

He greeted them.
He listened to them.
He shared with them his joy
of knowing the Father.
He helped them whenever he could.
That is how Jesus gave his life
for us every day.

at the last supper, beautiful

Jesus gave us the most sign of his friendship

Before Jesus died, he wanted to celebrate a special meal with his friends.
That night he told them some very important things:

"The Father loves you."

(John 16:27)

"I came so that you may have life."

(John 10:10)

"The Father will send you the Holy Spirit."

(adapted from John 14:16)

47

20

in the Eucharist, we celebrate the Father's and Jesus' love

At Mass, we offer our life
to the Father with Jesus.

To offer our life means to try,
like Jesus, to live for others.
United to him, we give joy to the Father.

To celebrate the wonders
of the Father's love,
the priest opens his arms wide and says:
  ''Let us give thanks to the Lord our God ''

We can say:
  ''Praise the Father,
    the Son and the Holy Spirit
    both now and forever.''

21.

Jesus asks us
to love one another

Sometimes it's hard to love; we don't feel like it,
we are tired or in a bad mood . . .

But Jesus tells us:
  ''If anyone wants to be my friend,
   let him take up his cross and follow me.''

   (Matthew 10:38)

Do I understand these words of the Lord?

Lord Jesus, give me your Spirit
so that I may have the courage
to love even when it's hard to love.

53

22.

are we always faithful to Jesus ?

At the Eucharist, Christians
remind themselves that they have
sometimes been selfish or mean.
But they put their trust
in Jesus who says:
    ''I came for sinners.''

Then each one says to the Lord:
    ''I confess to almighty God
    and to you, my brothers
    and sisters,
    that I have sinned.''

23.

Sometimes we tease each other and we
fight just for fun, but at other times
we hurt each other and cause pain . . . .

When that happens,
what does Jesus ask of us?

Jesus asks us to forgive

and be reconciled

"Happy are those who make peace;
they will be called children of God."

Open my heart to your word.
Teach me the joy of keeping your law.

24.
happy are those who are called to the Lord's supper

When we eat together, it means we are friends. God our Father invites us to this special meal because he loves us. He wants to unite us to himself and help us to live together like brothers.

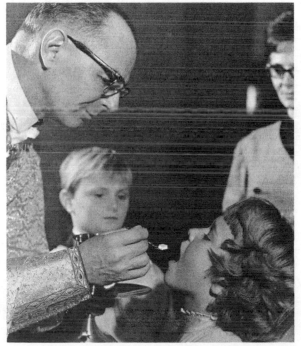

25.

at Mass, we eat the bread of life

To live, to grow,
and to be strong, we share
the bread of men every day.

To live as children of God
and to grow in love,
we need the bread of God.

Jesus has said:
"I am the bread of life.
  Whoever eats this bread
  will live closely
  united to me.
  Whoever eats this bread
  will live forever."

(adapted from John 6:35, 56, 58)

26.

Jesus is our savior

"Yes, God loved the world so much
that he gave his only Son
so that all men
might be saved by him."
(adapted from John 3:16)

Christians often bow before the cross
or put flowers in front of it.
　　Why?
The cross reminds them
of Jesus' great love, and that
he gave his life for us.

27.

Jesus shares his risen life

Jesus tells us:
"I am the living bread.
Anyone who eats this bread
will live forever,
and I will raise him up
on the last day."

(John 6:51, 54)

Rejoice, rejoice! Jesus is risen,
risen in glory from the dead.
ALLELUIA!

(Song 16)

28. the risen Jesus shows himself to his friends

The risen Jesus dies no more.
Someday we'll rise again
just as he did!

When the disciples of Emmaus
saw Jesus share the bread,
they recognized him.
They understood that
Jesus was alive and that he
was there with them.

When we share the bread of life
at Mass, we, too, understand
that Jesus is with us.

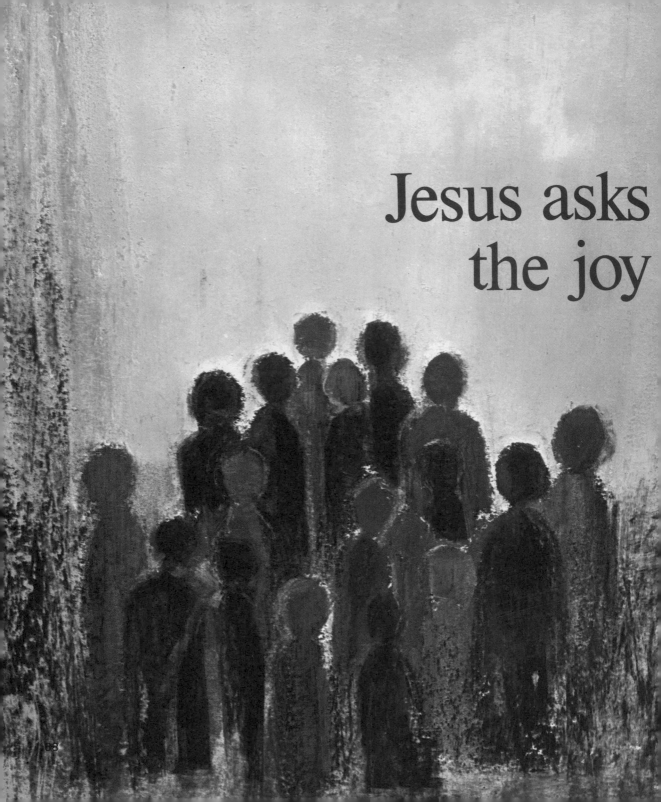

Jesus asks
the joy

29.

his friends to share of the Good News

After Jesus had gone, his friends gathered together and thought about his words. Little by little, the Holy Spirit helped them understand that they were to be the light of the world, that they were to share the joy of the Good News with all the people in the world.

Praise the Lord, all the peoples of the earth. Let all the nations give him honor.

who are Christians?

where is the Church of Jesus?

The Church is in every place where men
believe in Jesus, and try
to live like brothers.

Christians are just like other people, but
they have a great hope in their hearts:

> They know the love of the Father.
> They believe in the risen Jesus.
> They are closely united to one another
> by the Holy Spirit.

31.

why do we go to Mass?

To listen to the word of God.
To give thanks to the Father
with Jesus.
To share the bread of life.

God himself gathers us together
by the bond of his Spirit.

When we eat the same bread,
may the same divine love
unite us to all our brothers,
and unite us to our Father.

32.

hurray for vacation !

God loves our joy,
and he invites us
to share it with others.

What can I do
so that those around me
will be happy?

How can I remember
to help daddy and mommy
have a good vacation too?

32₂

God our Father,
it's you who make me live.
I want to sing your praises!

We give you thanks, O Father,
through your Son
Jesus Christ,
with the Spirit of love.
Amen.

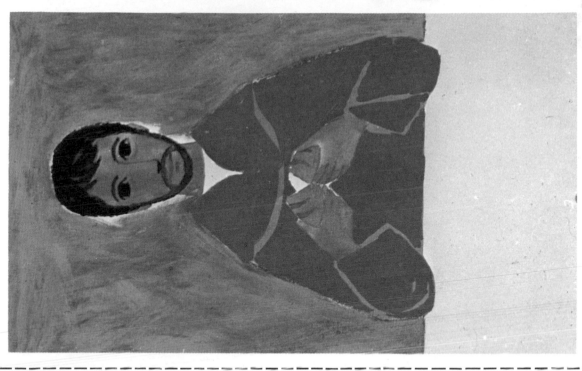

Philippe JOUDIOU

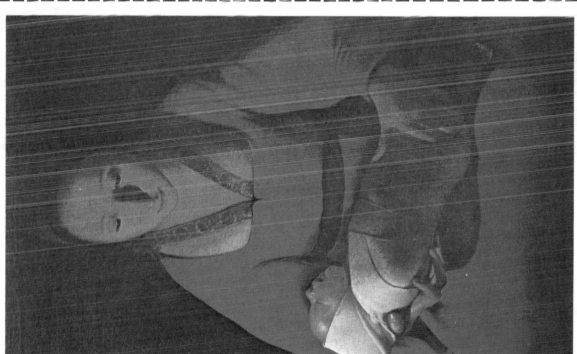

Georges DE LA TOUR